# My First Picture Bible

Retold by Sophie Piper

Illustrated by Emily Bolam

LION
CHILDREN'S

# CONTENTS

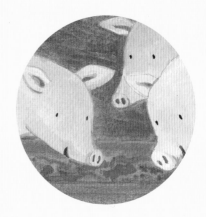

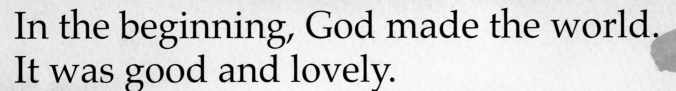

# Noah and the ark

In the beginning, God made the world.
It was good and lovely.

4

But the people made a big mistake.
They chose to do bad things.

Only Noah lived as God wanted.

God spoke to Noah.

"I want you to build an ark:
the biggest boat ever."

So Noah and his sons
set to work.

Noah's wife started to gather food.
Her sons' wives were eager to help.

They needed lots and lots and LOTS
of food.

Food for all the animals: a mother and a father of every kind of animal.

13

Two by two they came.

When everyone was safe on board,
God sent the rain.

The flood lasted for weeks and weeks.

Until…

BUMP!

One day the ark crunched on a
mountaintop.

As the flood trickled away, Noah sent
a raven to look for land. It never came
back.

Then Noah sent out a dove.

It came back with a fresh, green twig.

Somewhere, plants were growing.

When the land was dry, Noah opened the ark.

It was time to start the world again.

21

"Thank you, God, for keeping us safe," said Noah.

"Look at the rainbow," said God.

"When you see it, remember my promise:
I will never flood the earth like that
again."

# Moses and his sister

Outside the house, the soldiers came stomping: the soldiers of the king of Egypt.

24

"Shh," said the baby's mother.

"Shhhh," said the baby's sister, Miriam.

"We're slave people. The king doesn't like us. If the soldiers found the baby, they'd throw him in the river," whispered the mother.

"But we've made a boat out of a basket," said Miriam. "We're going to hide him.

"I'll watch over him."

Oh dear! The king's daughter came to the river to bathe. She saw the baby in the basket.

Would she be as cruel as the king's soldiers?

Not at all. "Dear little baby," she said. "I shall keep you safe. I shall name you 'Moses'."

Miriam stepped forward. "I can find someone to look after him for you," she said.

Moses grew up a prince.

He saw the king's slaves.

He knew that he was really one of the slave people.

"I shan't let them be whipped!" he said.

But that got him into trouble. He ran away.

In the wild country, he saw a bush: it was on fire, but not burning. God spoke to him.

"Go to the cruel king of Egypt. Tell him to let my people go."

Moses went.

"God says this: 'Let my people go!'" he told the king.

"No," came the answer.

"There'll be trouble," warned Moses.

And there was trouble.

All sorts of trouble.

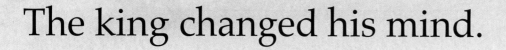

The king changed his mind.

"Take your people and GO!" he told Moses.

Everyone got ready.

They reached a wide sea.

Oh no! The king had sent soldiers to fetch them back!

God made a way through the sea.

Moses led the way. Miriam danced for joy.

God was their God. They were God's people.

# David, the shepherd boy

David was a shepherd boy.

Alone with his flock, he played his harp and sang made-up songs.

He spent his free time throwing stones with his sling.

Ping! He hit his target every time.

That was a good thing
if a bear came along…

or a LION!

One day he went to King Saul's battle camp.

He took homemade food for his soldier brothers.

King Saul's soldiers were lining up for battle when…

"HA HA
HA HA HA."

50

From the enemy side came a wicked laugh.

"I am Goliath," boomed a voice.

"Who dares to come and fight?"

King Saul's soldiers ran away.

David's brothers explained: "King Saul will give a big reward to the person who beats Goliath.

"But who dares?"

"I do," said David.

"Little brat!" said his brothers.

News of David's boast spread.

King Saul asked to see him.

"Oh," he said. "You're a boy.

"Goliath has been a champion soldier for years."

"I have my sling!" said David.

"I've killed a lion.

"And anyway: I trust in God."

"Hmm," said Saul.

"Well, at least wear my armour."

"It's too heavy," said David. "I'll go in my normal clothes."

He took his sling.

He walked down to a stream.

He picked up five stones.

He walked up to Goliath.

Ping!
David's stone hit Goliath.

HE HAD WON.

David grew up to be a soldier.
He became king after Saul.

He always trusted in God.

He sang this song:

*Dear God, you are my shepherd,*
*You give me all I need,*
*You take me where the grass is green*
*And I can safely feed.*

*You take me where the water*
*Is calm and cool and clear.*
*And there I rest and know I'm safe*
*For you are always near.*

# Jonah and the what?

Jonah was a prophet. He told people the things God told him.

One day God said, "Here's a message for the city of Nineveh.

"Go and tell the people there to stop their wicked ways."

Jonah went the other way.

He got on a boat.

"I will not go to Nineveh," he said.

"I want God to punish the wicked people there."

A storm blew up.

"Help," cried the sailors.

"This is the worst storm ever.

"Someone here has done something BAD."

Jonah had to own up.

"I'm running away from God," he wailed.

"Throw me in the sea, and you'll be safe."

Sploosh!

71

Down sank Jonah. Then...

GULP

He'd been swallowed by… a what?

"I'm sorry, God," wailed Jonah.

"If you save my life, I'll do what you asked."

Glob!

Suddenly Jonah was on the beach.

He hurried to Nineveh.

"Listen up!" he cried. "God says this: 'Stop being wicked… or else.'"

"Oh dear," said the people.

"Oh dear," said the king. "Listen, everyone: all wicked things must STOP."

Jonah went out of the city to watch from a hill.

What would God do?

Nothing. Nothing, nothing, nothing.

The sun was hot.

"I'm miserable," he wailed to God.

God woke a seed.

The plant gave cool shade.

"Aaaah," smiled Jonah.

God sent a worm.

Chew, chew, chew.

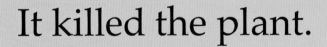

It killed the plant.

"Oh no!" wailed Jonah. "Waaaaaaah."

"I see you care about your plant," said God.

"Well, I care about people: the people of Nineveh."

# Daniel and the Lions

The three men scowled.

"How annoying," they agreed.

"Daniel got the top job."

"Let's get him."

They made a plan. They went to the king.

"O Great and Wonderful King," they said.

"You are greater than anyone in heaven or on earth."

The king liked that.

"Make a new law," said the men.

"Make it a crime for anyone to put their trust in anyone else on earth or in heaven."

The king liked that.

"And anyone who disobeys must be thrown to the lions," said the men.

"I'll make the law at once," said the king.

The men went to spy on Daniel.

YES! There he was, as ever. Saying prayers to his God.

"GOTCHA!" they cried.

91

They marched Daniel to the king.

"He prayed to his God."

"You must throw him to the lions."

"Oh," said the king. "Daniel's my top man. The law isn't about him."

"Your laws CANNOT be broken by ANYONE," said the men.

Daniel was thrown into a pit of lions.

The king spent a sleepless night worrying about Daniel.

97

In the morning he went to the pit.

"Daniel," he called. "Are you all right?
Did your God hear your prayers?"

He listened.

Prrrrr PRRRRRRR prrr.

He called again.

"Daniel!"

"Hello!" said Daniel.

"I'm fine. God sent an angel to look after me."

Prrrrr

PRRRR prrr

100

"Quick," said the king to his soldiers.
"Rescue Daniel AT ONCE!"

prrrrrrr

"I will tell everyone about this," said the king to Daniel.

"Your God is the most wonderful God in all of heaven.

"As for the men who tried to have you eaten… I have just the punishment."

MUNCH MUNCH MUNCH

# Little baby Jesus

The angel Gabriel was in Nazareth.

"I have important news," said the angel to Mary.

"God has chosen you to be the mother of his Son, Jesus.

"He will bring God's blessing to the world."

"I will do as God wants," said Mary.

The news made Joseph glum.

"Mary's baby is not my baby," he worried. "Perhaps our wedding is off."

In a dream an angel whispered:
"God has chosen you to take care
of Mary AND her baby."

Joseph was glad.

"We will be a family," he told Mary.

"Now I have to go to Bethlehem, for the emperor's People Count.

"Let's go together."
They set out.

There were lots of people in Bethlehem.

The inn was full.

Mary and Joseph made themselves cosy in a stable.

"Perhaps my baby will be born here," said Mary.

Out on the hills, shepherds were watching their sheep.

An angel appeared.

"Good news," said the angel.

"Tonight, in Bethlehem, a baby has been born.

"He will bring God's blessing to the world."

The shepherds found Mary and Joseph and little baby Jesus, just as the angel had said.

115

From far away, wise men came riding.

"There is the star," they said. "The sign
that a new king has been born."

In Jerusalem they found King Herod.

Herod wasn't happy to hear about
a new king.

Still, it was Herod who sent the men to Bethlehem. The star lit the way.

There they found Mary and little baby Jesus.

They gave their gifts:
gold, frankincense,
and myrrh.

When the wise men had gone, an angel whispered to Joseph:

"King Herod wants to harm the newborn king.

"Take your family to safety, far away."

It was a long time before Joseph and Mary and Jesus went home to Nazareth.

There Jesus grew up safely.

One day, he would bring God's blessing to the world.

# Jesus and the storm

Jesus grew up in Nazareth.

He helped at home.

He helped in the workshop.

He went to school.

He learned the stories in the holy books,
about God's love and care.

Even clever teachers were surprised at how much he knew.

127

When Jesus was grown up, he went to be baptized in the River Jordan.

It was a sign he wanted to begin something new.

He became a teacher.

People from all around Lake Galilee came to listen as he told of God's love and care.

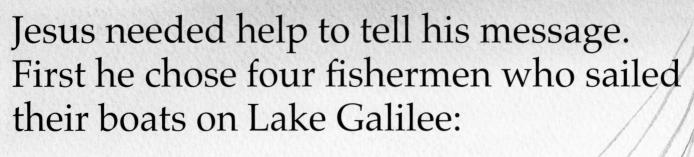

Jesus needed help to tell his message.
First he chose four fishermen who sailed
their boats on Lake Galilee:

Peter and his brother Andrew.
James and his brother John.

They left their fishing nets to follow him.

In all, he chose twelve people to be his disciples. Together they sailed to all the little towns on the shores of Lake Galilee.

The twelve listened as he told his stories.

The twelve watched him heal people with just a touch.

One evening, they all got into a boat to sail across Lake Galilee to another town.

Jesus fell asleep.

A storm blew up.

"Help!" cried the disciples. "Help us, Jesus! We're sinking down!"

Jesus stood up. "Be still," he said to the wind.

To the waves he said, "Lie down."

At once the lake was calm.

"Who is this Jesus?" asked the disciples.
"Who can he be, to do such things?"

# Jesus and the little girl

Down by the lake shore, Jairus was waiting.

"Hurry up, boat," he said to himself.

At last the boat arrived, bringing Jesus and his disciples.

Jairus rushed up to Jesus.

"Please help me," he said. "My little girl is very ill.

"Please come and make her well."

"Of course I will," replied Jesus.

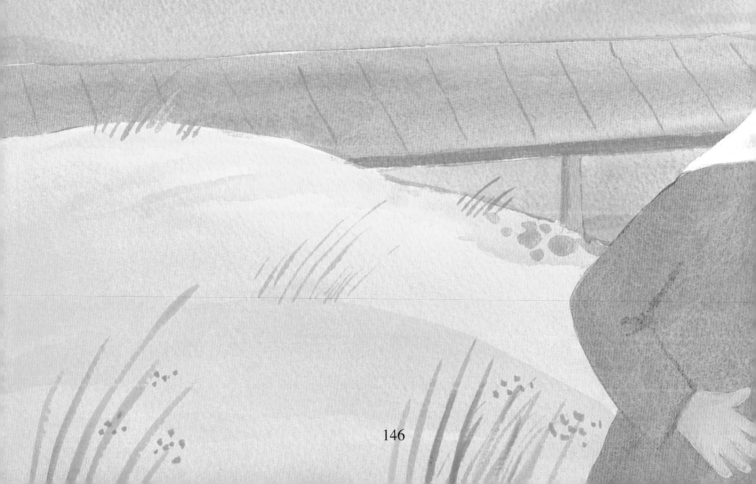

The street was crowded.

"Please hurry," said Jairus.

Then Jesus stopped. "Someone touched me," he said. "Who was it?"

The disciple named Peter laughed.

"Who knows!" he said. "Everyone's pushing and shoving to get nearer to you."

"I mean, who touched me to be healed?" said Jesus.

"It was me," said a woman. "I've been unwell for ages."

"Not any more," said Jesus. "Your faith has made you well."

As Jesus walked on, a servant rushed up to Jairus.

"Sad news," he whispered. "It's too late for Jesus to help.

"Your little girl… she's just died."

Jairus began to sob.

"Don't cry!" said Jesus. "Now you need to have faith too."

He walked on to Jairus's house. Outside, people were weeping and wailing.

"There's no need for all that," said Jesus.

"The little girl isn't dead. She's just asleep."

He went inside the house, with Peter, John, and James, and with the mother and the father.

He went to the room where the girl lay on a bed.

"Little girl, get up," he said.

At once she did!

Jairus and his wife were so happy.

"No need for words," said Jesus, as he left. "Just give your little girl something to eat."

# Jesus' story of the forgiving father

Jesus wanted people to understand what God is like. He told this story.

There was once a man who had two sons. Together they worked on the farm.

The younger son wanted to go his own way.

He went to his father.

"I want my share of the family money and I want it now!" he said.

"I don't think that's wise," said the father.

But the son kept on nagging.

In the end he got his way. He went to a big city far away.

He spent his money on all kinds of things:

fancy,

frivolous,

and fun.

He spent all he had.

He was left with no friends,
and no money,
and no way of buying food to eat.

He got a job: looking after pigs.

The farmer didn't pay him properly.

He was left so hungry that he even wanted to eat the pig food.

Then he had an idea.

"My father looks after his servants properly.

"I shall go back home. I shall say I'm sorry.

"I shall ask to be hired as a worker."

So he set out.

His father saw him from far away.

He came running to hug his son.

"Welcome back!" he cried.

He called to the servants: "Let's get this lad ready for a party."

It was a great party.

The other son was in the fields, working.

"What's the noise?" he asked a servant.

"It's a party for your brother. He's come home."

The elder brother scowled.

The father came out.

"That's so unfair," said the elder brother. "You don't treat me like this!"

"Everything I own is yours," said the father. "But it's really good news that your brother has come back.

"He was lost; now he is found."

"What is more," Jesus told his followers, "God is your loving father.

"When you pray, say this:

"Our Father in heaven,
hallowed be your name,
your kingdom come,
your will be done,
on earth as in heaven.
Give us today our daily bread.
Forgive us our sins
as we forgive those who sin against us.
Lead us not into temptation
but deliver us from evil."

# Jesus' story of the good Samaritan

All kinds of people loved to listen to Jesus.

But what he said made some people angry.

"How dare he call himself a teacher!"

"We're teachers and we know better."

"Let's ask him a really hard question."

One of the teachers went to ask: "What must I do to please God?"

"What do the holy books say?" Jesus answered.

"Love God, and love your neighbour," answered the teacher.

"Quite right," said Jesus. "You knew already."

"But who is my neighbour?" asked the man. Jesus told a story.

There was once a man who was going from Jerusalem to Jericho.

Robbers jumped out and beat him up.

They took all he had.

They left him in the road.

A priest from the Temple in Jerusalem came by.

He saw the man. He saw that he was hurt.

But he simply walked by on the other side of the road.

A helper from the Temple in Jerusalem came by.

He saw the man.

He walked closer to look.

Then he too hurried on by.

A Samaritan came by.

Jesus waited a moment. No one liked Samaritans. They had funny ideas about God. They had nothing to do with the Temple.

Jesus continued.

The Samaritan stopped.

He went and helped the man.

He took him to an inn and made sure he was all right.

The next day he had to leave. He gave the innkeeper two coins.

"Please look after the man who was beaten up," he said. "If it costs you more, I'll pay next time I come by."

201

Jesus smiled at the teacher.

"Now I have a question for you," he said.

"Who was a neighbour to the man?"

"The one who was kind to him," came the answer.

"Then you go and do the same," said Jesus.

"Remember this," Jesus told his followers.

"You are to love everyone, even the people who are mean to you.

"Go out of your way to be kind and helpful and generous."

# Jesus and the cross

It was festival time. Jesus and his disciples were on the way to the Temple in Jerusalem.

"Hooray," shouted the crowds.

They waved palm branches.

"Hooray for the king."

That made the teachers angry.

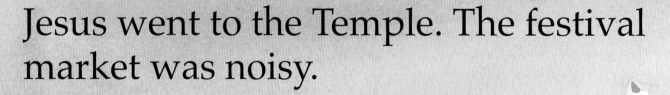

Jesus went to the Temple. The festival market was noisy.

Jesus tipped over the tables.

208

"Stop all this buying and selling," he said. "This is a place to pray."

That made the Temple priests angry.

The priests and the teachers got together. "Let's get rid of Jesus," they agreed.

One of Jesus' followers came to them in secret.

"If you pay me, I'll help you," said Judas.

The time came for the festival meal.

Jesus broke the bread for his disciples and shared it around.

He poured the wine.

"I want you always to share a meal like this," he said, "and to remember me."

Then they went to an olive grove, to sleep under the stars.

Judas went a different way.

He arrived later... bringing soldiers.

They marched Jesus away to the priests and teachers.

"We think your teaching is all wrong," they said. "You're in trouble now."

They told lies about Jesus to the man in charge, Pontius Pilate.

Pilate gave the order for Jesus to be nailed to a cross.

Before he died, he said these words: "Father, forgive them."

As the day ended, some friends came and laid him in a tomb.

They rolled the stone door shut.

The sun set.

Through all the next day, Jesus' friends wept.

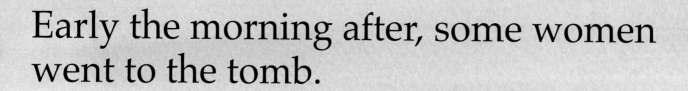

Early the morning after, some women went to the tomb.

The door was open.

Angels told them amazing news: Jesus was alive.

His friends saw him many times.

"I am going to heaven," said Jesus.

"Now I want you to tell people about God and God's love.

"I am opening the way for everyone to come into God's kingdom."

Text by Sophie Piper
Illustrations copyright © 2016 Emily Bolam
This edition copyright © 2016 Lion Hudson

The right of Emily Bolam to be identified as the illustrator of this work has been asserted by her in accordance with the Copyright, Designs and Patents Act 1988.

Published by Lion Children's Books
an imprint of
**Lion Hudson plc**
Wilkinson House, Jordan Hill Road,
Oxford OX2 8DR, England
www.lionhudson.com / lionchildrens

ISBN 978 0 7459 6551 2

First edition 2016

**Acknowledgments**

Bible extracts are taken or adapted from the Good News Bible © 1994 published by the Bible Societies / HarperCollins Publishers Ltd UK, Good News Bible © American Bible Society 1966, 1971, 1976, 1992. Used with permission.

The Lord's Prayer (p. 183) as it appears in *Common Worship: Services and Prayers for the Church of England* (Church House Publishing, 2000) is copyright © The English Language Liturgical Consultation and is reproduced by permission of the publisher.

A catalogue record for this book is available from the British Library

Printed and bound in China, July 2016, LH25